GEMINI

This Book Belongs To

_____

GEMINI

The Sign of the Twins
May 22 – June 21

By Teresa Celsi
and Michael Yawney

Ariel Books

Andrews and McMeel
Kansas City

GEMINI

ISBN: 0–8362–3073–6
Library of Congress Catalog Card Number: 93-73367

Contents

Astrology

An Introduction

Early in our history, as human-kind changed from hunter-gatherers to farmers, they left the forests and moved to the plains, where they could raise plants and live-stock. While they guarded their animals at night, the herders gazed up at the sky. They watched the stars circle Earth, counted the days between moons, and perceived an order in the universe.

Astrology was born as a way of finding a meaningful relationship between the movements of the heavens and the events on Earth. Astrologers believe that the celestial dance of planets affects our personalities and destinies. In order to better understand these forces, an astrologer creates a chart, which is like a snapshot of the heavens at the time of your birth. Each planet—Mercury, Venus, Mars, Jupiter, Saturn, Uranus, Neptune, and Pluto—has influence on you. So does the place of your birth.

The most important element in a chart is your sun sign, commonly known as your astrological sign. There are twelve signs of the zodiac, a belt of sky encircling Earth that is divided into twelve zones. Whichever zone the sun was in at your time of birth determines your sun sign. Your sun sign influences conscious behavior. Your moon sign influences unconscious behavior. (This book deals only with sun signs. To find your moon sign, you must look in a reference book or consult an astrologer.)

Each sign is categorized under one of the four elements: *fire*, *earth*, *air*, or *water*. Fire signs (Aries, Leo, and Sagittarius) are creative and somewhat self-centered. Earth signs (Taurus, Virgo, and Capricorn) are steady and desire material things. Air signs (Gemini, Libra, and Aquarius) are clever and intellectual.

Water signs (Cancer, Scorpio, and Pisces) are emotional and empathetic.

Each sign has one of three qualities—*cardinal*, *fixed*, or *mutable*—which shows how it operates. Cardinal signs (Aries, Cancer, Libra, and Capricorn) use their energy to lead in a direct, forceful way. Fixed signs (Taurus, Leo, Scorpio, and Aquarius) harness energy and use it to organize and consolidate. Mutable signs (Gemini, Virgo, Sagittarius, and Pisces) use energy to transform and change.

Every sign has a different combination of an element and a quality. When the positions of all the twelve planets are added to a chart, you can begin to appreciate the complexity of each individual. Astrology does not simplify people by shoving them into twelve personality boxes; rather, the details of your chart will be amazingly complex, inspiring the same awe those early herders must have felt while gazing up into the mystery of the heavens.

The Sign of the Twins

In Greek mythology, the constellation Gemini was created by Zeus, the king of the gods, to honor the twins Castor and Pollux. Their mother was Leda, queen of Sparta; however, Castor was the mortal son of Sparta's king, and Pollux was the immortal son of Zeus.

The twins were famous as great warriors. In life they were inseparable, but mortal Castor was destined to die. Heartbroken, Pollux begged Zeus to let him die so he could join his brother. Zeus compromised, requiring from then on that the twins be apart—each would spend half his time on Mt. Olympus, the other half in Hades.

Gemini reflects the duality of the sign under which it is born, often seeming to be two people. Gemini sometimes can be mortal Castor, concerned with the material world, and sometimes be immortal Pollux, living in the spiritual realm of Olympus. But whether Castor or Pollux, Gemini appears always to be searching for its twin—for its other self.

Character and Personality

You are passing a car lot when you decide to stop and just take a look. The next thing you know, you are ordering the latest model with all the extras. Chances are good that the charming, articulate salesperson is a Gemini.

Gemini has a dazzling mastery of language. It is the embodiment of diplomacy, wit, and compelling attractiveness. But it's often difficult to find the real Gemini beneath the glossy surface. While Gemini can easily charm others into telling all, it also uses the flash to hide its true self from the world. The sign of the Twins is usually wary of revealing a deep-felt sense of loneliness or of something missing—the way twins feel when they are apart.

Gemini is the sign of communication, and those born under it do best when expressing themselves verbally. For example, a Gemini student will find hitting the books and sitting through lectures tedious. The best way for the Twins to learn and exchange ideas is through a lively discussion.

Of all the zodiac signs, Gemini is probably the most unpredictable. One minute it is all sunshine and good cheer, the next, ice and cynicism. The sign of the Twins is capable of quickly shifting moods and attitudes, a reflection of the duality of its personality.

Boredom is Gemini's greatest enemy. Working for hours at one task is torture for the Twins, who delights in doing more than one thing at a time. Solving a crossword puzzle while talking on the telephone is a breeze for Gemini.

Gemini has a quick and curious mind, and might be distracted from one idea or course of action by another, more appealing one. Gemini may be late for appointments, skim books (or skip to the end), or hastily finish one conversation in order to move on to a new topic. This allows Gemini to cover a lot of ground, but prevents it from delving below the surface.

At heart, Geminis are explorers whose goal is to investigate the whole of creation. No wonder they tend to skim the details—they have a large area to cover! Since humankind has yet to build a ship capable of reaching the stars, Geminis will have to use their minds to carry them to the farthest reaches of the galaxy—and a Gemini mind can be a powerful vehicle.

Signs and Symbols

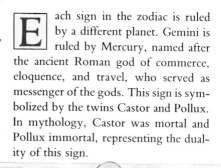

Each sign in the zodiac is ruled by a different planet. Gemini is ruled by Mercury, named after the ancient Roman god of commerce, eloquence, and travel, who served as messenger of the gods. This sign is symbolized by the twins Castor and Pollux. In mythology, Castor was mortal and Pollux immortal, representing the duality of this sign.

The third sign of the zodiac, Gemini combines the element of air (intelligence) with the mutable quality of transforming energy. Witty, versatile, forthright, and sometimes superficial, Gemini is a brilliant, inventive thinker, essentially an explorer.

Gemini rules the shoulders, arms, hands, lungs, and nerves and is linked with Wednesday. Its lucky number is seven, and its animals are small birds, monkeys, and butterflies. Yellow is this sign's color, crystal and beryl are its gemstones, and mercury is its metal. Its plants are ferns, myrtle, jasmine, and grafted trees, and its foods are grains and carrots.

Health and Fitness

The sign of the Twins fairly vibrates with energy. The typical Gemini talks, moves, eats, and thinks faster than others. It needs plenty of rest and nourishment to replenish the considerable energy it expends each day. However, many Geminis suffer from insomnia and are inclined to neglect their diet.

Gemini rules the shoulders, arms,

hands, nerves, and lungs, so those areas are often susceptible to illness or stress.

Gemini is also very vulnerable to its surroundings, particularly its emotional environment. Gemini suffers from indigestion and can actually worry itself sick. The Twins can also become prone to accidents when emotionally on edge.

Because this sign is inclined to fret, Gemini suffers more from inactivity and boredom than from overstimulation. It benefits most from a varied fitness program—for example, alternating a group sport like softball with an individual exercise like swimming. Whatever the activity, the Twins need fresh air to keep the blood circulating.

Home and Family

To Geminis, home is not exactly a castle, it's more like an endless cocktail party. Geminis love to socialize. And the Twins welcomes newcomers as eagerly as they do their inner circle of friends.

Nonparty days seem to have the same hectic quality. Gemini loves unexpected occurences, even when they interfere with regular household tasks.

Even without distractions, Geminis do not always excel in taking care of the house. If it's a small problem, like fixing the washer in the kitchen faucet, then Gemini can do it. But because Gemini is not typically persistent or patient, bigger jobs like painting might be too much.

Gemini's changeability can sometimes be confusing for loved ones. For example, disciplining children is not Gemini's forte—behavior that's punished one day might be allowed the next. But Gemini can focus on its strong points to be a loving, entertaining, communicative partner and parent.

Careers and Goals

Although Gemini has the talent, intelligence, and energy to succeed in just about any job, the communications field is especially compatible with the Twins' verbal fluency, mental brilliance, and incessant curiosity. Writing, politics, public relations, advertising, and the media are naturals for Gemini. John F. Kennedy, Judy Garland, and Walt Whitman are three famous and talented Geminis. The Twins also lean toward engineering, electronics, and aviation.

Gemini thrives in offices where the atmosphere is especially social. This sign's ability to do more than one task at a time serves it well in an environment where versatility is required.

Geminis are excellent project supervisors since they are good at generating ideas and then planning their execution. There is no one like a Gemini supervisor to shake up a department. Don't, however, expect to find the Twins sitting in a corner office. Geminis hate being enclosed; they want to mingle and network.

For Gemini, sitting around with friends telling jokes, gossiping, or talking about nothing in particular is satisfying and fun. Self-expression and the witty exchange of ideas are the ultimate goals of any Gemini activity.

Gemini loves party games, especially those like bridge or Pictionary, in which it can interact with a partner. It doesn't really care who wins or loses. All the Twins want is a chance to sharpen its wits in the company of intelligent equals.

As children, Geminis quickly learn to read, and their love for the written word continues throughout their lives. Geminis are sure to have many different and changing interests. They may pursue one hobby for a while then drop it and begin another with equal enthusiasm and facility.

Puzzles, riddles, and conundrums fascinate Geminis since their innate sense of logic gives them an edge. With their quick reflexes and mental alertness, they are also terrific at video and computer games.

Love Among the Signs

W hat is attraction? What is love? Throughout the centuries, science has tried and failed to come up with a satisfying explanation for the mysterious connection between two people.

For the astrologer, the answer is clear. The position of the planets at the time of your birth creates a pattern that influences you throughout your lifetime.

When your pattern meets another person's, the two of you might clash or harmonize.

Why this mysterious connection occurs can be explored only by completing charts for both individuals. But even if the chemistry is there, will it be a happy relationship? Will it last? No one can tell for certain.

Every relationship requires give-and-take, and an awareness of the sun sign relationships can help with this process. The sun sign influences conscious behavior. Does your lover catalog the items in the medicine cabinet? Chances are you have a Virgo on your hands. Do you like to spend your weekends running while your lover wants to play Scrabble? This could be an Aries-Gemini combination.

To discover more about your relationship, find out your lover's sun sign and look under the appropriate combination. You may learn things you had never even suspected.

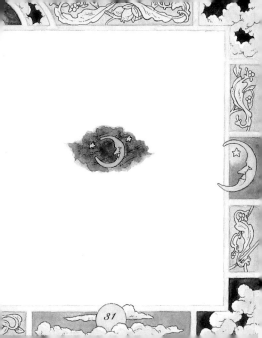

Gemini with Aries
(March 21–April 20)

A ries, the sign of the Ram, is a cardinal fire sign ruled by Mars, the symbol of energy. When the Ram meets the Twins—one of the most freedom-loving, versatile, and quick-witted signs of the zodiac—sparks fly.

Like the Twins, the Ram loves new people and new experiences and hates routine. These signs also have a mutual fear of commitment. Each harbors secret fantasies of leaving its lover and running away—someday. Gemini yearns for "the road not taken" and imagines that if only its job or spouse or home were different, it would be richer, healthier, and happier. Aries imagines that a more "perfect" partner is just around the corner—if only the Ram were free.

Such fantasies can persist even after many years of a happy relationship. The tendency to shun commitment doesn't arise from any lack of love; rather, it is the result of uncertainties about the future. Fortunately, neither of these signs is afraid to show its feelings to its partner and can openly express its fears, knowing the other will understand.

Two opposing qualities—Aries' aggressive straightforwardness and Gemini's tendency to deliberate—will cause conflicts between these signs. The Ram always plunges full steam ahead, preferring a bad decision to no decision. To Gemini, Aries seems somewhat simple-minded in its directness. On the other hand, the Twins cannot choose an outfit or order from a menu without stopping several times to consider the consequences. In exasperation, Aries may view Gemini as indecisive. These signs are not likely to keep anything bottled up, but they must remember to discuss their frustrations with each other—not with their friends.

The bedroom is where Gemini and Aries are most compatible. Gemini thinks of sex as a game that will delight its partner with imaginative loveplay. For Aries, lovemaking is a passionate expression of feelings that cannot be put into words. This combination of Gemini's imagination and Aries' passion gives both partners the variety and spontaneity they need for a long-lasting relationship—even beyond the bedroom.

Gemini with Taurus
(April 21–May 21)

G emini and Taurus have little in common. To quicksilver Gemini, Taurus is positively ponderous. Air sign Gemini wants action, and to experiment with new ideas and people. The sign of the Bull is a fixed earth sign that craves stability and security and dreads change. However, stability and security are qualities Gemini is short on—and always seeking. The Bull can give these, as well as intense devotion, in abundance.

Nevertheless, Gemini should consider whether it is ready to settle down. Taurus is a long-term partner who doesn't fall in love often, and certainly doesn't fall out of love easily. If Gemini starts something with Taurus, it should be prepared for commitment.

This relationship can grow if each sign will deal with its own contradictions: Gemini loves new challenges but longs for security; Taurus stubbornly resists change, all the while harboring a desire for excitement and adventure.

Gemini can benefit from Taurus's predictability. For example, the Bull is loathe to leave its familiar comfortable home, and the Twins, who tends to wear itself out, could use a restful evening now and then. For Taurus, too much of the same thing can make it morose. Gemini offers Taurus a tantalizing walk through the world of new ideas. The Bull may not want to dwell there, though it is thrilled to drop in periodically.

A business relationship between these two could work if each handles a different task. Let Taurus take care of the money: The Bull has a firm grasp of the material and knows how to make financial gains. The Twins can deal with the creative side and communications and may learn the value of patience and perseverance from Taurus.

As lovers or spouses, the Bull and the Twins can have problems. Taurus is an intense, possessive lover, at times almost stifling. The Twins sees lovemaking as a playful game, and requires the stimulus of attachments outside the partnership. While these may be friendships or harmless flirtations, the Bull may take them as evidence that Gemini is lacking in love and loyalty.

Compromise and communication are important to this pairing. If each sign vows to accommodate the other's needs, they can have a lasting relationship, with Taurus offering a safe home for Gemini to return to after restless wanderings.

Gemini with Gemini

(May 22–June 21)

S ince it is sometimes difficult for Gemini, the sign of the twins, to find and settle down with a compatible partner, why shouldn't it try mating with its double? On the surface, this seems like an ideal pairing: two quick-witted, charming adventurers off to explore the world, welcoming new ideas and experiences together. Underneath this surface compatibility, however, lie many pitfalls.

If Gemini expects to establish a stable, mature environment with its twin, it could be disappointed. Such a partnership can sometimes resemble a mental version of a sword fight. (Remember, the Gemini twins, Castor and Pollux, were renowned as warriors.) In the case of two Geminis, this takes the form of verbal sparring rather than physical combat. But they won't just argue: these two mutable air signs will delight in finding someone who can match them in intellect. Two Geminis can talk for hours, discussing every imaginable topic, including their romantic feelings for each other.

But even with all that sparkling conversation, there is always something held back. Gemini has a secret self it almost never reveals, even to its nearest and dearest. Others may not sense this since Gemini cleverly ducks most questions. A twin, however, can.

The Twins' most deeply guarded secret is a sense of inner emptiness. Gemini's lifelong exploring and investigating is often an attempt to fill this emptiness. In the search for something it feels is missing in its life, the Twins can sometimes become overwhelmingly lonely. No one understands this as well as another Gemini. Not only can a Gemini detect this feeling in its partner, he or she knows just how to steer the loved one away from depression.

Two Geminis need to bring emotional depth to their relationship and get past their cool, detached exteriors, or they may not develop close or lasting ties. With that depth, they can discover in each other hidden reserves of compassion, good humor, and even trust. With prize attributes like these to uncover, a Gemini is more than a bargain to its twin partner—it will be a treasure whose worth is beyond calculation.

Gemini with Cancer
(June 22–July 23)

Gemini will be attracted immediately to the mysterious Cancer. The Twins, however, should be warned: The basic difference between these signs is that Gemini thinks and Cancer feels.

Cancer is a cardinal water sign, ruled by the moon, the symbol of moods and emotion. Gemini, a mutable air sign, lives in the realm of ideas and experiences. The Crab's mysteries can defy solution and may only become deeper when probed. Delving into the secrets beneath that shell, the Twin sign may find itself in over its head.

The main conflicts in this relationship will grow out of Gemini's flirtatiousness and Cancer's possessiveness. Cancer does not make friends so much as it engulfs them. The Crab, who can find an entire universe in its loved one, cannot understand Gemini's need for others and fears separation. What Gemini simply regards as amusement, Cancer sees as betrayal. Although the Crab may forgive Gemini's indiscretions, it will never forget them and can carry the wounds for a long time.

Money can also be a point of friction between this pair. If, however, the emotional relationship is fulfilling, financial conflicts will not be major. Emotional security is more important to the Crab than financial stability. And a rewarding relationship will restrain Gemini, who tends to overspend when bored.

Sex between these two will never be boring. Cancer's moods vary wildly with the phases of the moon, and so will the Crab's lovemaking. Gemini may wish to introduce innovations but must proceed cautiously. Cancer is willing to learn new things but only in a safe environment.

Gemini will switch its personality

with the snap of a finger. Cancer will run the gamut of moods from joy to sorrow with stunning intensity. These two can weather these ups and downs by accepting that their life together will be an emotional roller coaster.

They should also try to balance each other's moods. When Cancer is blue, Gemini can offer a comforting shoulder. When Gemini falls prey to nervousness, Cancer should embrace the Twins with a circle of serenity. Thus these two can last by taking turns supporting each other.

Gemini with Leo

(July 24–August 23)

Essentially a wanderer, Gemini still requires a stable home where it can rest. So much traveling takes its toll, and the sign of the Twins needs calm surroundings the way a helicopter needs a level landing spot. Otherwise, Gemini will constantly hover.

A fixed cardinal sign, Leo can surround Gemini with serenity. Ruled by the sun, the Lion, symbol of Leo, is warm and comforting. What the Lion requires in return is admiration and loyalty. Leo the monarch's friends and lovers are its subjects. If Gemini is willing to go along, this relationship will work out.

That's not to say this combination won't have its sticky moments. Although a smooth, flattering courtier, Gemini can eventually tire of playing the part for Leo. And if the Lion, who tends to be bossy and arrogant, becomes too overbearing, Gemini might well slip off to play with someone else for a while, a terrible blow to the Lion's pride. Knowing it is not the center of Gemini's universe can arouse Leo's anger and jealousy. Then Gemini may be exiled from the Lion's heart.

Another danger is that Gemini will become too comfortable as a courtier, causing the relationship to degenerate into a mutual admiration society. While this may feel good to both parties, it can block them from further growth. To solve this problem, Gemini might use its natural inventiveness to take the lead and introduce some new games. The trick is to establish a balance between comfort and stimulation.

Physical relations are an area that can generate tension. To Leo, lovemaking is an all-consuming expression of adoration and passion. For Gemini, it's an amusing game. One part of the Twins may sit back and observe the action while the other part is involved. Leo will sense that Gemini is less than absorbed and may interpret it as dissatisfaction. If Leo thinks its love is not being taken seriously, the Lion will feel inadequate and hurt. Gemini should reassure Leo by revealing its sincere affection.

This is a pairing that can provide satisfaction and happiness for both signs. Charming Gemini intrigues and pleases Leo, and the Lion is not threatened by the Twins' wandering nature as long as it knows it rules Gemini's heart.

Gemini with Virgo

(August 24–September 23)

A s steady, sensible souls, earth signs provide the safe, stable environment Gemini craves. For the Twins, however, finding an earth sign that can deal with its mercurial personality is hard.

Of the earth signs, Virgo is best able to understand Gemini's behavior. Like the Twins, Virgo is mutable, and the sign of the Virgin also shares Gemini's ruling planet, Mercury, which influences communication. These two have a facility with words.

Virgo, however, uses language to analyze and clarify; Gemini creates illusion and fantasy with language to express itself. Virgo's conversations with the giddy Gemini are often frustrating. Every time Virgo pins down an idea, Gemini destroys it with a quip or a pun, like one child scattering another's patiently built house of cards. If the Virgin will keep a sense of humor, it will find discussions with the Twins intelligent and illuminating.

Virgo is an ideal partner and roommate, genuinely considerate of those around it. Virgo is a sign of service to others, whether on a grand scale or on a more modest one, and is at its best when tending to a loved one.

Unfortunately, Virgo's obsession with the smallest practical details can drive Gemini crazy. If any of Virgo's carefully arranged possessions has been moved, Virgo will put it back with a bang to let Gemini know it's disturbed the order of things. If Gemini comes home late for dinner, Virgo will be smoldering with silent disapproval.

Gemini can try to explain, but Virgo sees through all the Twins' tricks. With devastating precision, the Virgin will analyze the situation and point out exactly

where Gemini is wrong and how Gemini's behavior reflects fundamental personality flaws. Nothing is worse than enduring a tongue lashing from a Virgo.

Most of the time, however, Gemini and Virgo make a compatible partnership. Virgo will not party as often as Gemini would like, though the Virgin will not object if Gemini goes out alone. A typical Virgo does not suffer from jealousy as other earth signs do, since it is not a reasonable emotion. And Gemini could decide to stay home. After all, with a Virgo, the Twins is blessed with both stability and stimulation—just what Gemini craves, in one neat package.

Gemini with Libra

(September 24–October 23)

For good looks, good humor, and just plain charm, there is no better pair than Gemini and Libra. Libra is a cardinal air sign ruled by Venus, the planet of love and affection. For Libra, whose symbol is the Scales, life must be harmonious and in a perpetual state of equilibrium.

These air signs share much the same outlook on life. Both value ideas and thought over feelings and emotion. Neither sign will expect a heavy, emotional relationship from the other.

Libra may be a bit jealous of the Twins' restless quest for the stimulation it gets from other people. The Scales should be careful not to let its desire to be part of a couple turn into possessiveness. Besides, just a bit of enticement from Libra can keep Gemini at home. No one is more intriguing to Gemini than the joyous, intelligent Libra.

Gemini, although changeable, values stability in a partner, and the Twins might be put off by Libra's mood changes. To achieve emotional equilibrium, the Scales often swings wildly back and forth. In its need to balance every element of life, Libra often can be indecisive and lacking in purpose. Eager to please, Gemini will eventually learn to relax with Libra's obsession for equalizing.

These two are in their element at social gatherings: Gemini will see that food and drink are plentiful; Libra will make sure that the decorations are tasteful and the guest list has the proper mix of personalities for stimulating conversation.

There is nothing these two cannot talk out—and talk they will. Like other air signs, these two often use conversation and argument to define their own opinions. Outsiders may see these arguments as obstacles to the relationship. To Gemini and Libra, they *are* the relationship.

As lovers, they will talk as much as they will kiss. Both will be content to experience sex as a pleasant pastime rather than a passionate expression of love. Libra will seek harmony in the relationship, and Gemini will fulfill the Scales' desire to be loved. Together, these two can achieve the balance between security and freedom they both need.

Gemini with Scorpio

(October 24–November 22)

S ome sun signs click immediately and combine without a hitch— but not these two. For Gemini and Scorpio to stay together, compromise is essential.

Scorpio, whose symbol is the Scorpion, is characterized by deep intensity, passion, and the will to survive. A fixed water sign, it signifies the capacity to transform and change life. At times the

Scorpion can be like quicksand, drawing others into its world and overwhelming them.

Air sign Gemini has no fear of Scorpio's intensity; Gemini doesn't mind being seduced. However, if Scorpio demands commitment before Gemini is ready, the Twins will run away. If Scorpio can relax its iron grip, Gemini will come around—at its own pace. Scorpio's endurance and magnetism fascinate the Twins. Gemini dwells in the bright, sunny air, and Scorpio's deep, dark watery depths are a whole new area of exploration.

Once involved with Scorpio, however, Gemini will have to rethink its lifestyle. Scorpio lives by strict rules, one of which is "Thou shalt not suddenly become another person." Being a sign that represents the power of transformation, Scorpio can accept change only if it is serious and controlled. And of course, Gemini is the most changeable sign in the zodiac.

If Gemini is not careful, it can violate Scorpio's rules without even realizing it. For example, Gemini does not exactly lie, but it has a cozy relationship with language that allows it to take liberties. Stretching the truth horrifies Scorpio, to whom such flexibility breaks all the rules.

Perhaps no other sign embodies so

much sexual magnetism as Scorpio. Though a passionate lover, the Scorpion also can be a possessive and jealous one. Gemini's lighthearted lovemaking will not be attractive to Scorpio, who will try with all its might to hold Gemini to a serious commitment. Whether as married partners or as lovers, Gemini must focus on Scorpio and not be distracted by other potential relationships.

If Gemini can be flexible, both these sun signs will be rewarded. In a committed relationship, Scorpio can provide the stability Gemini needs for its ultimate well-being. By allowing Gemini more freedom, the Scorpion can find the deep love it craves.

Gemini with Sagittarius

(November 23–December 21)

K eeping up with fast-talking, fast-thinking Gemini is a chore for most people, but not for Sagittarius. This fire sign might not be as graceful as Gemini, but it is just as quick.

At opposite ends of the zodiac, these mutable signs can either balance each other's qualities or drive each other crazy. Sagittarius, the sign of the Archer, is full of enthusiasm, optimism, and ideas. If this pair click, they can unite the Archer's concern for eternal truths and universal knowledge with the Twins' concern for information—gathering it, discussing it, and communicating it.

Conflict will arise over differing perceptions of truth. Sagittarius is the most honest sign of the zodiac. Gemini sees truth as relative and can change from pro to con in a snap. The Archer sees truth bending as dishonest; Gemini thinks Sagittarius is naive.

Sagittarius is a highly inventive conversationalist who can match Gemini quip for quip. With such a chain reaction of creative energy, these two can exhaust a subject in minutes, at which point they will quickly turn to another. Although Gemini admires Sagittarius's wisdom and knowledge, the Twins often wishes the Archer were less idealistic and a bit more realistic. In turn, Sagittarius is excited by Gemini's creative use of knowledge but finds the Twins' superficiality and nervous energy exasperating.

These signs both need a stable, neat environment. Unfortunately, neither is good at providing that, for themselves or for others. Both view cooking and household chores as wasted effort.

Still, the pair is well matched. As a visionary, the Archer can lose sight of the details. Gemini will be delighted to supply them. The Archer's honesty will help Gemini restrain its tendency to bend the truth to its own advantage.

Gemini and Sagittarius will be clever, exciting lovemates. Sagittarius enjoys an imaginative and spontaneous sex life and can be a demanding lover whom Gemini is happy to accommodate. As their relationship grows, calm will replace combustion. And instead of creating sparks, they will fit together as smoothly as watch gears.

Gemini with Capricorn
(December 22–January 20)

O rganized and conservative, Capricorn, a cardinal sign, is the authority figure of the zodiac. Ruled by the planet Saturn, even the most congenial Capricorns have an almost forbidding air of formality. Always working or getting ready to work, ambitious Capricorn couldn't be more different from the fun-loving Gemini.

Reality exists for Capricorn, an earth

sign, in the tangible material world. The sign of the Goat doesn't trust abstract concepts. To Gemini, even daydreaming is living in the real world. It is futile for Capricorn to try to convince Gemini otherwise.

Gemini is a charming salesperson. In business, this selling ability, as well as Gemini's limitless flow of ideas, could benefit Capricorn. Down-to-earth Capricorn can help Gemini organize its brilliant but scattered energies. In fact, a business partnership may be the best kind for these two.

A personal relationship will need a lot of work. These signs have different senses of humor, attitudes toward work, ways of communicating, and sexual needs. Gemini will benefit from the relationship since the Goat will always be a good provider. But the Twins should be ready for the silent treatment if there are disagreements. Discussing an issue calmly may be difficult for the flighty Twins, but this will help communications with the serious Capricorn.

Though neither sign is cold and without passion, lovemaking is another area where Gemini and Capricorn may have trouble connecting. Capricorn relates to a lover primarily through the senses. Gemini, however, needs mental as well as physical stimulation. Further tensions can come about if the Goat takes seriously Gemini's tendency to flirt and becomes jealous.

Gemini may decide to leave Capricorn behind while it explores the universe of the imagination. The typical Goat is too earthbound to soar with the Twins. Traveling solo in the universe can get lonely, and eventually Gemini may decide to stay closer to home. How well a relationship works between Gemini and Capricorn depends on how willing each is to adapt to the other's nature.

Gemini with Aquarius

(January 21–February 19)

When Gemini and Aquarius meet, these two will probably become best buddies. Like Gemini, Aquarius is an air sign and tends to experience the world intellectually. Unlike Gemini, Aquarius, whose symbol is the Water Bearer, is a fixed sign. It is ruled by Saturn, the planet of reason and uniqueness. The Water Bearer wants to investigate the world and to learn its natural patterns. Aquarius is a true scientist, forming theories, conducting experiments, and verifying the results.

In almost all ways, Gemini and Aquarius are well matched. They are quick-witted intellectuals who love to discuss and hash over everything. Both are social signs who attract a variety of friends and acquaintances. In fact, they share a need for the stimulation they get from other people and from new experiences. Neither is jealous nor possessive. And neither will make emotional demands on the other.

However, as their relationship progresses, the Water Bearer and the Twins will discover an odd discrepancy in the ways they view the world. Aquarius seeks an underlying truth to the universe and wants to reduce life to a set of provable mathematical equations. Gemini, on the other hand, is well aware of life's duality. The sign of the Twins does not need to reconcile seemingly contradictory information—Gemini embodies many contradictions and can allow such complexity in the world around it as well.

Even though Aquarius will view Gemini's point of view as utter nonsense, the Water Bearer can't help but admire Gemini's brilliant, sharp mind and quick wit. If the two can focus on the compatibility they have in other areas, Aquarius may try to understand Cemini's point of view and learn to relax its rigid standards a little.

Sexually, these two signs are more comfortable living in the realm of ideas than in the world of emotions. They may have so much fun talking that they remain platonic friends and never get around to a romantic relationship. But if they do, they may discover and explore the world of emotional and physical expression—together.

Gemini with Pisces

(February 20–March 20)

emini is a creature of the air; Pisces, the sign of the Fish, belongs to the watery depths. Although both Gemini and Pisces are mutable signs, Gemini is air and Pisces is water. Since Gemini soars above the clouds and Pisces dives to the bottom of the ocean, these two may have to work hard to find someplace between their two elements where they can both be happy.

Pisces will find it difficult to understand Gemini's need to be with a variety of people. Pisces will find emotional fulfillment in one deep relationship rather than a hundred shallow ones. What the Fish must learn is Gemini needs the mental stimulation it can get only from many experiences. Crowds are as necessary to Gemini's well-being as love and emotional fulfillment is to Pisces.

On the surface these signs seem to have some characteristics in common, but what motivates them is not at all similar. They are both changeable, but for different reasons. Pisces lives in the world of emotions and feelings. The Fish is totally in tune with its emotional environment, and everything it does changes according to the moods it senses.

Gemini follows its own mysterious pattern of movement. The Twins can hardly sit still for five minutes. At a party, Gemini will dart from group to group, interacting quickly and then moving on, sipping stimulation from each person like a hummingbird sipping nectar from a flower.

Because of a basic difference in how each communicates, they will both have to listen carefully in order to understand each other. Gemini expresses itself intellectually, with words and ideas; Pisces uses its imagination and emotions to make contact with others. Their signals are bound to get mixed up sometimes.

Patience is the key to this relationship. Each must try to see the world through its partner's eyes. This is easier for Gemini than for Pisces. A bird can dive, but a fish can't fly—and the Twins will need to go more than halfway. The enlightenment that comes from uniting with someone with such a different perspective, however, is the reward Gemini will reap for its efforts.

The text of this book was set in Bembo
and the display in Caslon Open Face
by Crane Typesetting Service, Inc.,
West Barnstable, Massachusetts.

Book design and illustrations by
JUDITH A. STAGNITTO